Sergei Kuzmich from All Sides

LETTER MACHINE EDITIONS SEATTLE, WA

Sergei Kuzmich from All Sides

Jessica Laser

Published by Letter Machine Editions
Seattle, Washington

Cover Art: Alécio de Andrade
left: The Adoration of the Shepherds with Saint Benedict, 1552-1554. Girolamo Mazzola Bedoli.
right: The Circumcision, 1590. Federico Fiori Barocci, known as Baroccio.
Louvre Museum, Paris, 1993 (detail)

Book Design by HR Hegnauer
Printed in the USA
Cataloging-in-Publication Data is on file at the Library of Congress
ISBN: 978-1-7327721-0-6
lettermachine.org
Distributed to the trade by Small Press Distribution (spdbooks.org)

for my parents,
Joan and Gary Laser

Contents

Sergei Kuzmich from All Sides

Paradise Lost

In the ice cream parlor, Sergei pulled out a stack
of my marked up poems, words or their syllables
blacked out for rhythm, and told me it would happen for me,
that I was like a wild stallion he didn't want to lead
but follow, and that he recognized it was difficult
to believe those things about myself, so he would believe
them for me. Across the street, we attended the party
of a famous German writer, we'll call him
Sergei, whose novel had been turned into a movie.
Sergei was significantly older than I and I had accepted his
invitation to the party knowing the other guests would consider me
arm candy, so when he asked me to recite for the company
I relished the opportunity to prove I had a brain.
After the recitation, one of the guests, a trade fiction writer,
Sergei, took interest in me. He was impressed
by my memory and asked me questions about myself.
I was from Chicago and had recently arrived in Brooklyn,
where I lived in Greenpoint at 120 Milton, glad the recitation
had produced somebody besides Sergei with whom to speak.
He had an idea for me, which he prefaced with the statistic
that he rarely offered such advice to other writers and those
who took it succeeded invariably. He suggested that I spend
my time on Milton Street memorizing *Paradise Lost*, all ten books,
with the purpose of writing a memoir. This, according to Sergei,
would bring me fame and money. I was so heartbroken
at the time I seriously considered it. My coming into possession

of the copy I'm reading now dates from The Strand around then.
From the party, my housemate Sergei picked me up in my Prius,
which despite his preference for making car services wait
outside Zabar's while he shopped, he had borrowed to take
Maple to the beach. I said goodbye and thanks to my host
and then again to the doorman as he watched me leave.
When I had just arrived on Milton Street, Sergei came down
to meet me, twelve years my senior, hair salt and pepper,
pulled to a top-knot, the prevailing style at the time,
and helped me carry my stuff inside. Later, over Last Words
or caviar or tuna steaks he seared on each side in a thick layering
of salt and pepper, he helped me carry some other, less tangible
burdens I still haven't quite put down. At the time, he was such
a drunk he often slept under the bench in the backyard with the
cigarette butts he left there. I would see him from my window
in the morning. He was going through a divorce thick with
money and cheating. 120 Milton was all drunks except me
and I drank every day. Even Maple, Sergei's new girlfriend,
struck me as a drunk, but it may have just been that she was in
her early twenties. That night I saw her in nothing but a black bra
and panties, stark against her pale skin and red hair and I looked
away so quickly the contrast made her an equals sign.
I had gone upstairs to confront the music, the hour inhospitable
to such a racket, expecting to find the usual crew arrayed
around Sergei's third floor apartment in positions of repose
that bring to mind Raphael's *School of Athens*, particularly
Diogenes on the steps. Instead I found the two of them
alone, wasted, dancing to music enough for two hundred
people in the light of the early morning, Sergei shirtless and
Maple equal, the music so loud they didn't hear me

come in. I went downstairs again and thought of Sergei's
day, which from mine ended so differently, but began the same,
as he had driven me to the ice cream parlor where we were to meet
for a pre-party coffee; the party was across the street.

The Fish That Are the Whale

In the depression between two hills,
We rode at a walk. Gentlemen,
As you were, don't you see
Your fear came true? Life is not as cruel as you
And the crueler you consider life, the crueler you'll be.

We agree. I understand you completely
But I don't understand the way you treat me.
The people I've treated this way
I haven't loved. I don't understand
How you can love me the way you treat me.

In the patch of grass behind your house,
A neighbor crouched and waited.
We rode from the North and I said hi.
I had nothing to hide, though like a new bride
Or a cold one, I had covered myself with a sheet.

Where we rode, truth tellers hadn't heard of a lie.
They believed instead in delayed rhymes:
I can see your lips and eyes moving, but no words
Exit your mouth. Finally you tell me your thought.
By that time, it no longer rhymes.

We rode up and down and life kept pace,
Everyone me or a postcard
From a faraway place. Croatians
Called me "America the Beautiful"
But I prefer gorgeous.

Commas in Dante

Loosed from the rain, suspended
like a bough that broke and didn't fall,

Sergei returned to fix the fake fire.
I'd worried the pilot was on too strong.

Though he fixed it for free, fire
always means profit and free

in this case means already paid.
"Finally," I calculated,

"I found out I love you.
We achieved the physical

life of difference
we'd always held from each other inside.

I saw your life as if across a stage
I had tossed you a looking glass.

There are so many ways to think of us
that I have thought them all.

In one, we've been a painting
to which we were in a museum drawn,

stood peering at it for days
imagining the essays

and then we walked away.
In another, we preferred to dine

with literary people of unliterary sympathies,
who said at the restaurant, humiliating the effort,

Get your head out of books. Write for the waitress.
I close down around me like a thousand-petaled lotus

when I privilege my sympathy with others
over my system of belief, my thought

that at times I have no sympathy
at all, none except my own belief

that I have no belief
that is not a sympathy.

Freeing myself from what ailed me in others
gave me room to encounter someone new.

That's how I took you, as someone
working for but excluded by virtue."

"Makes me feel dumb,"
he said of my poem.

Fazana

When my woman says hello
She says what can I get you.

I had no time to peruse the menu.
I was lost in thought and English

Came last, after German, French,
And Dante with no mirror page.

I decided then that to eat
Would be fine, but to decide the dish

Translation. Croatia lost to Brazil.
I went to my room to make sure

Of everything, as I often needed.
There you were absurdly, suddenly

A parrot on my knee. Your plume
Fired in the background.

To see you
So upset me

I would have learned a new language
If it meant in English to disconnect my knee.

Between two other, similar versions
Not in the same translation

I found in myself the lyric I looked for.
I found it with its moral intact.

A poet must heat to song in the dark
Lest reckoned the pot he died to see boil.

Sergei

He irks the phone I could remove
And touch the water.
Man of what pebbles
The government pours

To adorn concrete lapping waves
Denote as slabbed beaches.
Views of an island so recently
Opened, no public generation has been.

Meeting the couple concrete
Ends of the dock, the man
Whose legs puncture water
Is in it. His islands

Dictate their two-story summer homes
To me, he says so,
"Now they will be no one's
Till the rich buy them up again."

These boundaries I OK.
If the islands were everyone's
We couldn't imagine them mine,
As we know to, something equal

To the being in possession of it.
While the sun is setting
The islands look honest—
Sullen lumps of sodden granite,

White as I think of them
Turning to think of something else,
To see if I can, if the man loves me.
I know he's been looking

And how I'm ashamed,
An island, slow-moving
Heat the sun sets apart.
I remove myself

At the pace of the spider.
I carry his burdens
Far as the sensation
Of ownership goes.

Tractatus

Every notary carries within him the debris of a poet.

1.

Of restrained instinct
I'll no longer be the candle

"In the dark?"
"Yes"
"Like, the *dark*?"
"Yeah"

Whose pennies come out
of a frost of expense

Whose heart is a basket
a rose to catch thorns

Whose casket a test
of whose love taught me how to

2.

You think we have the same
Sickness I think we have
The same health

It's nicer to get along
It's like making a decision
Very slowly, over many hours
To be alone

It's nice to be alone
It's like making a decision
Very slowly, over many hours
To be with others

3.

I deserved no pleasure
Went to sleep

And there is the upcoming tour
I'm leaving for

I can't cut this notary
But need to access his debris

I saw him under his sheets
Numbered—to correspond to his beds

I saw him number his soil
To correspond to his pots

His characters correspond to his plots

I saw that man make silt
Out of nothing, out of a little
Spot of clay—and the world drained
Poorly from my sight then, even when
I closed my eyes I saw man

4.

We are very kind
And like enduringly true facts
With non-exclusive truths
We are in love

But we did this for our grand advances
For in our departure

We wept a staggering sea

We are still in it

With silt

And of everyone

We left, he couldn't believe
What we thought of him, couldn't believe
That we thought of him at all

5.

A pilot mans his own ascent

Not to know
Not to fix
Man is whatever
He can afford to be

Within him, every poet

Carries debris

I locked those habits in a drawer
Where I was told they'd be

What is the difference
Between now and forgetting

And if I infer from the drawer
Will my inference be in it

I look at reason in the dark
It seems to me to flicker

Not the flame and not the wick
It is the motion to and fro

It could be both though

But, well, I don't think artists have particularly bright ideas. Matisse's Woman in Blue, Woman in a Red Blouse, *or something, you know — what an idea this is! Or the Cubists. When you think about it now, it is so silly to look at an object from many angles. It's very silly. It's good that they got those ideas because it is enough for some of them to become good artists.*

WILLEM DE KOONING

"So it never went further than 'Sergei Kuzmich?'" one lady asked.

"No, no, not a hair's breadth," Prince Vassily replied, laughing. "'Sergei Kuzmich. . .from all sides. From all sides, Sergei Kuzmich.' Poor Vyazmitinov just couldn't get any further. He took up the letter several more times, but as soon as he said 'Sergei'. . .sobs. . .'Ku. . .zmi. . .ch'— tears. . .and 'from all sides' was drowned in weeping, and he couldn't go on. And again his handkerchief, and again 'Sergei Kuzmich, from all sides,' and tears. . .so that they finally asked someone else to read it."

TOLSTOY

The Rock

I tried to chase the phantom.
I stood in it. I recognized a deficit
The problem located
In me or others
But in that the phantom
Could not be addressed
I reached out and it
Addressed itself to me.
Life is a process
A pretty glow from a lamp
A cloud glowers over
And troubles the phantom
Within that assumption.
So me I couldn't say what I received.
I was relieved. That was the phantom
And I the recipient
Could not be addressed but to it.

Sensual Delight in Virtue

Ciao ciao ciao ciao
Bella bella bella bella

I don't exist to appear
I exist to exist

This mass couldn't be anymore
On the radio

She is overlooking me
She is, it's true

She's looking for something that doesn't appear
She will one day make it visible

I don't exist to appear
I exist to exist

And I went there, too.

When a fly hurts, it scans
Where it might have flown
With weird optical versions
Of longing. Your body hurts
And hurts. When your mind
Hurts, it has thoughts

That hurt you. For example,
How could I divorce
Someone to whom I'm
Unwilling to pay alimony?
And I went there, too
Because I understanded.
I completed a family
Met along the river
As it levels out.

It was in this very depression
Between two hills
That I rode.

When I complete a family
We are never better, never
Than when our enemies love us
Which is to say when we fail.
But Sergei Kuzmich from all sides
There is no treason to describe.

When a fly hurts, it scans.
When your body hurts
It hurts. When your mind
Hurts, its thoughts
Hurt you. For example,
How could I divorce
Someone to whom I
Went there, too
Because I understanded,

I completed a family
Met along the river
As it levels out.

It was this very depression
Between two hills
That I straddled.

Gentlemen, I said *as you were*!
But she is overlooking me!
So she is! It's true! She's looking for something that doesn't appear
But one day she will make it visible
For though those arms are leprous as snow, it takes soft arms
To tear down fences, soft features
To exist to appear.

I exist to exist.
When I complete a family
We are never better, never
And our enemies love us.

In the Depression between Two Hills

Replacing myself into the calm
Seated body patiently awaiting
My replacement, I had recurring
Dreams that ended with me
Sitting up suddenly

In my bed, still in the dream,
From which I woke
Suddenly and sat up frightened
Of the repetition, as if of a glitch
Or a stutter.

It's like a stutter, my awareness,
Two sounds where
There should be one,
But two sounds
In awareness of their oneness.

In awareness of their oneness,
We rode at a walk. Gentlemen,
You talk too slow. You have
No sleeve to wipe your nose
And when the dawn breaks

Its colors upon you,
Which shall you absorb?
For men are pregnant all the time
With information.
Some with wisdom.

Assumed Knowledge and the Knowledge Assumed from Experience

The ring's thirst is in you: to reach itself again

Everything you say is wrong
Everything you say you do
You don't mean what you do
Not at all

Does life feel funny to you?
It does to me.
I'm chasing the good.
That's a feeling.
A promise.
Does it come to you?
It does to me to say so, not the good
Which is better.
Can I still care about your concerns?
I am concerned by what concerns are.
Are they yours?
Are you surprised?
Discerning people come through that door.
I said something you'd understand
So you'd see them
And understand it
And it was at the edge of your understanding.
You're describing the language you're using instead of the room.
—*The baby enters.*
People speak as they shouldn't.
They shouldn't be ashamed.

Considering your reputation repetition and duress
Something quick in the world moves with me
With pleasure if something quick at all
That's you in trouble
The body with spirits
I said to myself as a child do not
Mistake the ghost you fear for
The ghost you are
Flesh over time
To hold for the orators
Though it be elder
I learned in my danger
Myth in my youth
Those who attend pay others to
Build the climate rains on
Shacks of nets to cast where they are
Cast your nets where they are

Words mean to me
What are they mean to you
To include the cypress
Bark to her
All along as a dog

I'm naked without memories with me
Whose cars devise the soft cotton (sleep)
It was not to my calling
To crash on the plaza
Nor the mental respite in stone
What hurt you forgives

I don't take the medicine
Preferring to sit here
With anybody—music
And its rival
Sun

Take me to the place we'll call home.
I'll meet you.
Remove from me solace and sorrow.
Recline on me, it would be my rest.

I have faith and the faith has me.
We love the green puddles that form
The mud games by which
Grass
Closer to your pocket grows
And swims.
Blessed are the silent
For they need not bless.

God does not love your
Indifference. Goodbye.
For the deeper peer we seek.
Silence (our motto)
Omits our remove. It was what
You thought—you were wrong
The way you thought you were.
You were upset
About what you thought you were.
People profess a comforter
And darn pearls along the form.
We wear our coats for someone else's
Winter, who would not know we were cold.

The swings

The swings

The swings flee the intact faculties
Still the trees with them, loose
Looking like little lonesomes
Trying to enjoy the great festival of life with other men.
I stood where the standers lie
In Assyria
Like a collapsed house
Walking around from inside.
I had touched a man's arm and it hurt me.
There was a watch on it, an official of the state.
Where were we when you arrived on the scene?
What time did you arrive?
No I don't want to testify—I don't believe
Your honor I don't believe
The state proves this case against me.
I moved
To dismiss the case.
I saw a man's arm and it hurt me.
He had a watch on it.
You see how full of changes change is?
Was. Shouldn't they block it, send
Back all the things you
Slow so we die?
We will so we slow
The official's evidence.
Where I stood I dreamt
I was a pirate sea
With all beings and boats
In me legally arrested.
The night of the soul

They say, is of a level
Of horror unbearable to every man but
The mystic. When I saw the man, I
Lived unbearably. I had no vision
Of myself as a mystic,
No audience with god.
I read a mystic
Feels what I felt
So I touched, beneath the covers
People, having learned from me empathy
Enough to turn them down. "Throw him in prison!—
What prison?—Where he is already, for he is there."

What if I'm wrong
You're not wrong
What if there's something I didn't think of

Did you know you were making a miser
When the infant slow-babied the wild
To sit in a chair, the demonstration.
The moment in ammunition
All of a sudden
Echo so entry it's primary sound
Not just the ammunition
All loves enemy
And redress the ideal.
I love you. I love you
I love you I love you
And now I'll accept this.
Renderers press their garnet pall
Over the face swoops, down by the fire
A bird of four fathers, a band of four fathers
Echoes you into its fifth lagoon.

My mom is a shoulder
A person next to her
And next person too weak
To massage it.
This is a shadow of my mom.
How it orbits my being like.
Clumsy swan I am holding
Her neck up
And turneth myself to know
I would do.
Perfect. I would warp myself
Into the climax of an articulate gesture
To find there is no is in is
No sighting
Looks for life in bleak patterns
Guess what: a street
Can't forget
Its thoughts between the two white lines.

I called the opposites each other
I felt myself above myself
The audience could hear me clapping
Flesh over time
Wrong as I am
An industrial you
Makes all your mistakes
Conflates repetition duress with
Something quick and it moves in the wild
And slow with pain
And slope with plain

To employ your suffering
You must.

Here is the actual
Here it is actual
Incredible people
But what owl
So full of mice. . .

Once I was lonely
Someone of temperature
Concerned but not involved.
The marks I made measured
Against the wall
Each year rehyphenate
The wall to itself
For this is to show
Who can stand it.

To leave who's bad
Enough to leave
You must be bad
Enough to stay.

My friend believes he has what he deserves,
Believes desert derives from what he has.

To save who's bad
Enough to leave. . .

You must be bad enough to save.
No deity's instep to model a foot from,
Sharks keep on circling their prey.
Hence our moments
Open and flash the tide
Of our moments recedes
And died of our moments,
The good deed did.

Theirs are the germs of the human soul.
For who has not swum with sharks
Recoils in the rectangular fact
Of an existence containing many squares
And acquires the footage
Of a commercial living space
With porches.

You think you have to
Be perfect to watch it
When in fact
To employ your suffering
You must punish a child
With sleep.

You fall where you lie
And you sleep where you fall
But the logic
Travels its familiar strain over points
In time not space
And though you sever
You go on. Glass in a pond
Is what the sill would have you think
The logic empty of
And to empty the pond of it
Would belly up the mice one must.

We are what we have and memories
Keep us from comfort.
They are what we know.
You are what we know and I
I am the thing that knows you.

People apply
Their many logics.
They can't all be right
And are each wrong.
Two truths comprise our
O truths
Comprise our failures
And remember us.

Rule of Conflicting Desires

Yes there is more than one true love.
Yes but how devastating to be forced to know a second!
"Baby, shh, my regrets look like you."
"You may know what a baby means
 But I know a horse by his harness."

I downed my juice and walked home
By that one tree that incorporates the fence.
You said, "You made me do this."
"I wish I had so I could stop."
I wish you would sit next to me.
You have a chance and so does everybody
To value this, that though yours if you want to
I stood up too quickly to think of now.

He That Feareth Every Grass Must Not Piss in a Meadow

1.

With a second thought
At the head of the instrument
He by stringing made of the table
In shadowy rehearsals by lamplight
Unbroken, drawn up in day clothes
Lining the corn, the priest in snow
Traces the image he wanted back
To the dune defiled with grasses.

With a second thought
For love's thought to impede
The priest strings together
Love and denial, plays to
The dune defiled with grasses
That are not smart and do not love.

Alive in men I understand
What institutional feeling is.
I have the right to their existence
A madman has to love mankind.
My brother keeps a mower child
To shear the head love's thoughts defile
And mow around the intelligence those
Who are smart do not know.

2.

If that's what he's there for fine,
As long as it's what someone wanted.
Our Lady of Senses forgets she's all
She feels and seems and thinks to be
But distraught in that shame where is sin
She flocks to a shame that in glory and grace
Goes with everything, like a sofa with guests.

Welcome to Andover. A great deal of our
Witnesses long to know whether
The truth be in actions or staved off by them.
Any consciousness come into the universe
We shall labor to know only as
Hard as it labors to know itself.

She goes along like under guests.
Her weariness knows
No wickedness rests.
I set myself out tasks too great
To know myself and be a wife.
Until someone with beauty hands you your plate
The women will run
Ahead of the men asking their price.

Not fatigue nor knowledge of heaven
Could take away this sting of you
Contrasted with so many times
I was in ecstasy and wanted for grasp

For he's covering the cage
Or else a bear in it, a bar to it,
The illusory freedom
I wanted to give up.

That mother is a child's violin.

Because my god we all thought
A great deal of our witnesses
And longed for them to know the truth
By the actions we staved off in their presence
As times of day have complements
And colors opposites, consciousness
Comes to this world uninhibited
Like a dog that runs away

And like a horse it has the strength
To bear our freedom
And know in proportion
How hard it has labored
To free itself. As a horse
Bears gifts, it trusts what receives it.

A dog mimics intelligence
(Most when it runs away)
But noses ahead of itself the small animal
A woman runs up to
While her man asks after its price.
If he thinks of doing things that hurt her
The price will exceed a house.

Lord, give me strength.
I too have been thinking of you
Since the days war writers were generals
And we could hear them late at night
Laboring to keep their vows.
I miss them, cows for garrulousness
That did not milk but speak.

Furrow

I saw the furrow and my brow in it
Detaching itself from its mother arm
The bubble a vein trues
Inoculating against you.
In your fear, your child
Will contact whom you'd finally let go
For there is one who can attest as I
Having dug himself from me alive
And there is knowledge bored with stupidity
Loud as a cat's tongue scratching by flattery
Tulips the earth shoots up in solidarity
Request that he
Speak now or forever.

Late November Early March

You need not fear what peace you keep
And weak, what up against it comes
You come against the peace you seek
With keeping. Never fear.
The clothes on the line
Blow ghosts you unravel by their use.

This muddy spring clots with bits
Of stoneware ground beneath the fog
That spits and swirls your own.
Then cast clay cracks
A nearer sun
Through clouds than we thought.

You talk with a bit when you hold in your mouth
What's real or not
In subliminal autumn.
Then the tree rejects the leaves
And currents bear them each a load
To who can afford so high a treble.

We scan the naked bloated shore
With yellow eyes we carve along its span
And double the letter, pleased by its efface
And doubt the latter, placed by its effect
Which stamps the beauty from all sounds
And makes of its carrier a neck to ring

The parcel bag around and sue.
I carried food a long way from there
And sat beside the barrier as it rained
A fog so soft and clear
I thought the earth a mirror
And then it broke.

Stranger

He tooled around in the back shed, Greg,
While I took a bath in the watershed. In fact,
I trampled the whole series of flowerbeds—
Ours and those of our neighbors, whose
From ours are separated by a fence.
Tuning to the staticky dictionary, Greg
Listened for a definition of my condition
While tentatively I snorkeled
A remote, sparkling sea. Winter came.
I tied a sheet around our bed. Adrift
In deep melting ices, I tried to shun the obvious
And lost the ease I forewent. Did you take it?
I thought my homes better this way, stranger,
Engagements broken off for truer love,
And the fact that I live and someday won't
Made beautiful. How did you take them?
As a star in my allegiance glaring down?
Let that be light enough to turn it off.
Thoughts so permissible need not be had at all.

Against Doom

If you could capture doom and make it
beautiful, you'd make it icy like a sea.
You'd make the sky look up to it,
the rest of a wave under which we live.

At times there'd be no
sky at all, only sky
we wade in when we feel
we're what we see.

Doom is a planet, the views, the overhanging
vines and I live in a time of fruition,
obsessed with fun, feeling myself part of it,
a relic, a ruined thing.

The sky and sea are breaking.
The sun sets at a pace of ice
the ice itself is barred from.
Imagine you unite with what you see,

pain in a child, and that every unity
brings divisions as you cleave
from what you see ahead to meet it,
the child in pain.

The pace of the wave
we live under the crest of
the mind itself sets like a sea.
I try to unite my mind with me.

It rises like a setting,
a planet circling the nearest sun,
each sun a throat with hands around it,
this pain has nothing to do with me.

Modern Psychoanalytic Studies

According to my cousin Danny, because
I wasn't raised with the meditative tendency
I must transcend chronological experience
By methods aligned with, of my upbringing,
The speed and intensity. He's suggesting LSD
But the analyst at the lectern shouting
"Somebody should do something!"
To the knowing crowd who hears the wink
In his voice better than his voice itself
For the broken microphone is exactly
What somebody should be doing
Something about, and the child in the back row
Acknowledging rage, and the inscription
Handwritten into the front of the play
I'm reading while they fix the mike
Remind me I have taken in my life
Too much advice. I suppose I could take
Acid, too, but like a warped ladder,
Worn with use, leaned
Against a plentiful tree, the harvest
Of which grows only once
You've risked the climb,
I already know what it's like, and to know
What it's like is like being at work
Or vigilance, or a sentence
So beautiful that from it vigilance

Arises like a safe
From a jewel that's like being awake
For one of those reasons, the past
A reasonable hour.

Libido

Not a Hopper painting
but a photo of our street in
his day—horseshit covering
the unpaved way and "the pharmacy
in essentially the same place as today,"
my dull branch, too
wet to flame, is that olfactory
sense gone missing.
Our nose bleeds from the grief.
If any laughing soul became a circle
and swore to loop a dance all night
and roll it out like money carpets,
a person exiting would think to walk
Libido, the dog of wonders.
How quickly focus comes to view
the thing I'm looking at you through,
the thing I look away into.
You the telescope
take from my gaze, but a kaleidoscope
takes its place. I summer in its
triple vision, my calendar clothes
a clock on the wall. I love
to remember myself in that season,
bathing rarely, pining with each new hand,
my father calling about his will.
The conversation that ensued became

my inheritance: the way we discuss wills,
not what we put in them.
Still, my stairs differentiated then.
Suitors climbed until their souls went up
like pools committed to aerial memory,
a collection of laps, timed
to nations that form and disperse,
contraries they interview me toward.
Now, avoiding all obvious rising suns,
fist in my mouth, I am the West.

X-Men

Put, I pray thee, thy hand under my thigh

For it was the end we were looking for and not of the French.
We wanted to make the end most pleasing
To onlookers bulging (green from their minds).
Accused by a bishop laden with offenses
Of immutability, I spread the thing out you don't have
In your hands yet. So what, my beloved love. Who you give
In orders offense to. . .What dies before me I let rest.

With a dish on my breast, nickel-plated
And others I left blank for seconds
I accept the sum magnitude of this—
Two men, exiles each, come home from
The same country (abroad) only to find
That they keeping
Up the looks of emissaries
Pause to be at home
As spies in their own land.
The image required
Foraging here, not hanging there,
An heir (or two), a mountain view, and maintaining
The tenses as foreign gold you created of theirs.

And now this honeyed individual
Hides in the sun as you dry your true identity
Long with that patience just as wet when you ask

Your reflection to convey your mind
(Not my story) to the water
"I saw you chase them down"
"You saw me" "They ran" "We. . ."
Speaking in fast French (past tense)
To your countryman, a broken tongue rather
Than our language, as after a white man, even in private,
Assimilation you sought, because your future survived
The kind all undergo
After great grief
Back into the culture
That dreams its death in studded denim
Stretched tight over the thigh of a girl
It will never touch, who dreams culture
Could touch her.

Onyx Band

The onyx band relays your neck and head again
To ribs below and lungs flush against them.
"I took the blow for somebody else and it tied
My hair back with my neck still in it!"
So call me ground and all the more you fall.
You touch me when you're ready to posit
That down below consumption decks
The inner quarters and sleeps in his bed
On your behalf, those covers his
Eyes, for he's to thee a covering.

But don't look at me this way in ruins! I'm no
War postcard published in you (to be so crude).
She just wears what you bought her.
We don't have to remember that.
The June of shrugs decays its faithful side
When sliding down the back a bead
Of note plucks sweat before it
Dries to trails to lick to wet again.
He has a view on top as you
On your stomach shrug a fly loose.

Just saw them on the dock, the two
"I wanna go home and touch."
"I go home too much."
Not everybody likes to be touched.

He's so obsessed with the beautiful
Woman of you, he bought to subdue it
A necklace. The beautiful woman lives as you
Live to yourself when you are whom you lie to.
She will live with the lie having worked for her
And die when the lie gets old.

Ode to Persistence

after Juan Sánchez Peláez

In reality, without limit, but for measure and repose
The snake and the bee would give up their stings.
During the lecture on why, though the lit
Transparency seems incoherent, a lullaby
Threads its roots to the language
Rumoring them to grow as I describe.
Return the vessels through an immense
Shy body, littered with drunk evidence
If by drunkenness my evidence is
Brave enough to be of her, who opens up
The cover revealing my amulets accidentally
Guarded all this time against her
Because she was anonymous and they
Sought fame. Balancing my memory of her falling
Asleep in a sleepless phrase punctuated by bones
I lack diction. I would sleep but the human
Moment's an animal and to sleep is to vehemently
Shut the grand cage. I would wake the gold leaf
Adorning her cover, paralyzed but happy, pressed
As life to death, and face the years away from me
That worry on abysses formed where others fell
As I do for her by bullets from the arms we use
By usufruct, till she's too much, and when we have
To hand them back, she leaves deep imprints on our
Hands, where holding them we tried to grip the soul.

The Bulletproof Vest

The bulletproof vest should exist
In the bleary eyes of those who slept
As in your own house a voyeur
Shows you how to take it off
Convincing the whisper of steams to rise
From medieval mesh melted down to the armor
I think of as beauty, its arm around my mind.
I would take the immaculate climb
Over the ridges to see you
But the ridges are long
And we drove to their song
When down that coast-resembling road
We migrated south with the circus party
And laughed without nets.

Pretty my Petticoat Nearer my Smock

Though exaltation force regrets beneath its train
Gain goes recognized only in dank parlors
Where for fireplace we gamble away the name
And stoke our woe with sudden flame outcast.
Turns a mill to seep below employment
Each truss a carrier for one fell branch
That cycles down its weight to steward
Our climb most and hedge the torrent
Steadying the wicker polarizing to its drops.
I hear that licks the sky with nose intact
Can taste it, thus a shame saliva floods
Most the emotion it seeks to reform.
They tugging at my sleeves grow short and I want
To patch the end-unraveling maze (our help has quit)
And trip the one false bud that blooms the trees
And if our white shorts prove they are clean
To give them their past back, restoring
To earth the rain that redeems
Stuffing itself into each concrete basement
Slapping like poverty the face of life.

Tectonia

For the beautiful I opted out one evening
To see a street enraged in quiet
And what bore me never I thought to bear
But like an animal caged and rampant
I lifted life from its particular screen
And found the etchings marked decay
No sense of night my dwelling integrated
For it was upon these years I lay

And with great charm they bedded me as earth may bed in canyons
And if the word is not so big, enough to catch the sound
Nor open to its net the waving grain
Where I stand less faint—like a prison's grass—than grass
Resown I am begotten wicked
To will what has been seen once over
To hay in pleasant nearness to the corn
Or to imagine, once atop these boards, the sea
My weight the blunder of my passion
Until the planet being formal ropes in the world

King Lear

Pleasure abates overdoing.
Some skies blow farther overhead
And some hang
And some scream out of their way to be heard
But those are throatless and gentle
Who breach
Who find a cloudy adversary
To wilt below.

Subdue subdue
They'll scream at you.
The only kind is human.
No book bleeds like the reader.
No reader beats his book.

This or I Am That

It is wonderful to be angry
At someone I'll not see again.
The anger screams me back
To a time I'll never live through.
There is a table in that window.
There is a silence in the mind.
The table in silence produces
The window. The silent window
Produces the mind. There is a silence
In the mind, like a table setting
A table setting. There is a setting
On the table. There is a table
On the ground. I've found a coin:
The coin I found.

Thinking Differentiating Crashing

1. Definitions

The feather:
The part of the bird that does not decay.

The soul:
The part of the human that does not

Decay:
Knowing the soul we can know

Of the feather:
We can know only the soul.

2. Fish

Fish in a bowl
Aging without effort

Like to watch a long time
Obscured by people

Who wave.
The rest are displaced

Onto the water,
Into the heart of the viewer

Or elsewhere, for later.
If we strip them away

It looks like a woman.
No wonder it took two tries

To make her.

3. Addition

One has a wonder
Two imagine death
And they stone
A body I
Looked like
Once I thought oh
I thought
In order to think
In order to think
One must learn how
I could let you
Teach me how
If I could let you

4. Love

In love with complication
Wounded by urgency
Surmounting memory

Like a cresting ship
Elements compete
For spatial representation

If you don't hear me
Elements compete
For spatial representation

The dead compete
Within a definition of consciousness
That doesn't include them

And the stone over and what
I looked like when
I invented her I said oh she's

Oh she's not
What I thought

5.

There there was faith
Instead of god

And food
Instead of sleep.

The only good
Was forgiveness

Of evil
(Porchia).

The rain lasted
Only an hour,

The field
Only an acre,

But I never could tell a field from rain.

The Wave

The moving company called to tell me they had done me a favor—of the paintings they had wrapped and packed one hadn't made it into the storage container, which was to be fumigated against a pesky bedbug infestation that had gripped repeatedly my Brooklyn rental, so they fumigated it for free in a truck they were already fumigating. I told them they had spun their mistake into a favor and I was glad the painting wasn't lost. When I drove to Queens for the one free access they had promised, I found what I suspected: the painting that hadn't fit was the painting I came that day to retrieve, to give to its subject, who had asked to buy it from me. We hadn't spoken in years, but he had written with his request just as I was moving across the country with the intention of leaving the painting behind. I asked to make an exchange. I wanted a print of Courbet's *The Wave*, which once he had positioned just above the average person's head on our wall, the wave poised to crash over the viewer. The painting had a lifelike spirit, so that for the year it leaned against my wall in Brooklyn, people entering the room were startled by its unexpected presence. It was of a man reading, we'll call him Sergei, a man I had once known. At the storage access, I unpacked and unwrapped it. I lowered my car's back seats and laid the heavy wood panel flat over the car's entire back half and covered it with a yellow sheet, then drove back to Brooklyn where I parked in front of my building in preparation for the exchange. But Sergei never came. So I drove the painting around with me, refusing to give anyone a ride. I wouldn't bring the painting inside, though friends offered their places. I called its painter for advice. She said, "I hate that painting; leave it

on the street," but as I imagined propping the painting against a pole
on a corner, I saw in my rearview mirror Sergei reading as
I drove away and couldn't do it. I didn't feel comfortable parking.
I double-parked in front of my building and, lights blinking, ran up
to shower or eat. I slept in the car. I left the trunk open, hoping
someone would come and take the painting, but only
an auxiliary cord was ever stolen and instead of double-parking
I just kept driving and the highways passed me between them like
a family heirloom or spare key. I took 495 going east until it spilled me
onto NY-25 heading toward Orient Point, the northern tip of
Long Island where, when I arrived, I drove into a line
for the ferry to New London where I waited with every kind
of car, in every color, to load into the ship. I rolled my window
down and smelled the sea and felt the breeze. A gull on the roof
of the adjacent car flew away. I moved my car a few feet closer
to the bumper. People were leaving the little café with chips,
ice cream and soda water. The sun beat down. I paid a man
and drove into the cavernous interior that shaded our cars
from the summer heat. I felt the coolness settle. It was Sunday.
Suit jackets hung in the backseats of people returning from
a weekend at the beach. Some talked; some kissed; some listened
to the radio; some sat in silence; others read aloud.
Mothers soothed or ignored their babies. I turned on the news.
A man of extreme beliefs had proven himself the latest symptom
of a viral war that had no unified front but cropped up everywhere
as if emanating from a pulsing, energetic center deeper
than earth. The man had worn a bomb to a concert. Parents
had been waiting for their teenagers in the part of the arena where
he blew himself up and the shrapnel flew and mothers and virgins died
brutally, with nails in their backs and faces. In my side

mirror a dog's face peered from a window a few cars behind mine, its tongue hanging down. The ferry had long left the dock. I turned off my car and got out. I wasn't planning to look, but through the back window I caught a glimpse of Sergei where he lay, face up, sitting and reading. I opened the trunk and as I slid the painting from its place, a cascade of private phrases and pet names drowned all my thoughts and, afflicted with what Heraclitus would call a wet mind, I carried the painting through the aisle of cars, careful not to scrape their sides, to the front of the ship where people, alone or in small groups, let the wind wash over them. This same wind dried my mind. The ferry turned the water white. I leaned the painting on the railing and wished that I had brought a book or to be in the one Sergei was reading. I pressed with both hands the top of the painting to see if it would flip, then leaned beside it and reached for the water. I had brought a book. It was back in the car.

Losss

The reason why I lost my lamp was that the thief was superior to me in vigilance. He paid however this price for the lamp, that in exchange for it, he consented to become a thief: in exchange for it, to become faithless.

EPICTETUS

With tears in her voice[1]

With tears in her voice[2]

The important and the unimportant are the same only at the start[3]

The weak in courage is strong in cunning[4]

For a tear is an intellectual thing[5]

I am simple. I need not think. I must make myself felt and understood through feeling[6]

I will dance for institutions only because it makes it possible for me to express my personality[7]

I never verbalize about the dance as I create it. It is a purely physical risk that you desire to take and that you have to take[8]

(Costing not less than everything)[9]

I want to write this book in order to explain what feeling is[10]

I speak strongly on purpose in order to be better understood, and not in order to hurt people[11]

I have made mistakes but I corrected them with my life[12]

In order to read properly what one has written, one must think it again[13]

Thinking of Being is the original way of poetizing[14]

Thinking says what the truth of Being dictates[15]

O wretched minds, there is no gold that may
Grant that ye seek, no war, no peace, no strife
No, no although thy head were hooped with gold[16]

Each kind of life hath with him his disease[17]

Like rubies reddened by rubies reddening[18]

And for what, except for you, do I feel love?
Do I press the extremest book of the wisest man
Close to me, hidden in me day and night?[19]

Deep dove, placate you in your hiddenness[20]

Dispair[21]

While the narrowing rails slide together behind you[22]

Where nobody's waiting for us so they're not surprised[23]

It was honest for me to give my name[24]

Intimacy is gained but at the expense of illusion and nobility[25]

Space is the time you need to go to someone else[26]

It is hard to leap, mainly because we stand right on its edge. We are so near the abyss that we do not have an adequate runway for such a broad jump; we easily fall short[27]

I wish to hell he'd go home and fill up again. I wish to hell everybody'd go home[28]

The death of my father makes me feel as though I had written a beautiful book[29]

True, we love life, not because we are used to living but because we are used to loving[30]

A man in love with truth need not be either great or a poet. He is both without trying[31]

Poets and painters have leave to lie[32]

I never saw such a bunch of apple-eaters[33]

Behold, I send you forth as lambs among wolves[34]

That are like wolves these silly lambs among[35]

Who are only undefeated
Because we have gone on trying[36]

It is only by accident that you know someday how near a person has come[37]

Bringing this thing that has happened by accident to a much further point by will[38]

That's my drawback, that's my rigidness[39]

Thus, the basis of the capacity to be alone is a paradox; it is the experience of being alone while someone else is present[40]

Is it because the memory is more interesting or because the presence is disturbing?[41]

When you're outside a tradition, as every artist is today, one can only want to record one's own feelings about certain situations as closely to one's own nervous system as one possibly can[42]

I always feel like saying to music: "It isn't true! You lie!"[43]

It is the belief and not the god that counts[44]

God does not believe in our god[45]

Franny looked at what she could see of him[46]

Not see? Because of night perhaps?[47]

Effortlessly, by softening and thinning his voice, rather than by raising it to a falsetto[48]

Can't you see that? Can't you *see* how unclearly, how sloppily, you're looking at things? My God, there's absolutely nothing tenth-rate about you and yet you're up to your neck at this minute in tenth-rate thinking[49]

You don't face any facts[50]

I see a voice[51]

You are going to believe this[52]

I have crawled along the edges of plenty[53]

A peculiar exhaustion, I am so oppressed, doctor, set in[54]

The dream was bidding me to do what I was already doing, in the same way that the competitor in a race is bidden by the spectators to run when he is already running[55]

We were enjoined of old to learn to write now while young so that if we ever had anything to say later we would know how to say it. All there is to learning to write or talk is learning how to have something to say[56]

They will say that you are on the wrong road, if it is your own[57]

I am convinced that had he found more understanding, more gentleness, among those who surrounded him, including myself, he would have been spared the terrible mental anguish which eventually forced him to withdraw from the world of reality into a world of his own[58]

I have no defenses against these mourning necessities, which I found ridiculous when others observed them[59]

Nothing ends without breaking, because everything is endless[60]

Man, when he does not grieve, hardly exists[61]

For ruin and recovery alike are from within[62]

I have a gift for passion[63]

"You have an amazing work ethic."
"It's not an ethic; it's a habit."[64]

And if by grace, then is it no more of works: otherwise grace is no more grace. But if it be of works, then is it no more grace: otherwise work is no more work[65]

An effort to find fulfillment[66]

The purpose is beyond the end you figured
And is altered in fulfillment[67]

Being as being transcends objectivity[68]

Ontology speaks analogously[69]

The beginning of philosophy is to know the condition of one's own mind[70]

What you shun enduring yourself, attempt not to impose on others[71]

Socrates, when reminded that he should prepare for his trial, answered: "Thinkest thou not that I have been preparing for it all my life?"

"In what way?"

"I have maintained that which in me lay."[72]

Since obscurity is the privilege of young things[73]

"Well, here we are," he said, conscious that a young man would have said something different[74]

The emergency of the moment—the emergency of reading or talking[75]

What I am pointing out is that unless you are at home in the metaphor, unless you have had your proper poetical education in the metaphor, you are not safe anywhere[76]

Must I *drive* you to philosophy?[77]

Who will go drive with Fergus[78]

Bear and forbear[79]

Torture, exile, stripes[80]

Bear them we can, and if we can we must[81]

But we weary the unlearned, who need not know so much; and trouble the learned, who know it already[82]

We can do without faith. I should like to see a man suffering from doubt as he would suffer from an infected finger, and screaming with rage. Then I shall believe in moral suffering[83]

How can one be well. . .when one suffers morally? Is it possible to remain at ease in our time, if one has any feeling?[84]

He was accused by the bishop of London of a list of offenses that included treason and immortality[85]

Do we try men's faith by their persons? We should try their persons by their faith[86]

They were as interested in the question of how we ought to live as they were in the problem of the basic material out of which the physical world is made[87]

Look at everything that exists, and observe that it is already in dissolution and in change[88]

Games and their organization must be looked at as part of an attempt to forestall the frightening aspect of playing[89]

If everyone will listen to me, there will be no more war[90]

If everyone made war only according to his own convictions, there would be no war[91]

I have slain a man to my wounding; and a young man to my hurt[92]

And the Jebusite, and the Amorite, and the Girgasite,
And the Hivite, and the Arkite, and the Sinite,
And the Arvadite, and the Zemarite, and the Hamathite[93]

And note that his cruel extreme tyranny
That fedeth hym with my care and mysery[94]

Ah, mystery, Oh mystery
Why do you treat me so[95]

Oh, my Lolita, I have only words to play with![96]

The sentence must also contain its own apology for being spoken[97]

I and mine do not convince by arguments, similes, rhymes,
We convince by our presence[98]

A person may be in solitary confinement and yet not be able to be alone. How greatly he must suffer is beyond imagination[99]

Love beginnith at itself[100]

It is better coming to the end of a feast than the beginning of a fray[101]

There is time for all things[102]

I had rather have it now than twice as much another time[103]

Playing can be said to reach its own saturation point, which refers to the capacity to contain experience[104]

Being able to enjoy being alone with another person who is also alone is itself an experience of health[105]

Rostov passed by them, involuntarily noticing that one of them was covered with blood and rode on. "It's none of my business!" he thought[106]

Life meanwhile, people's real life with its essential concerns of health, illness, work, rest, with its concerns of thought, learning, poetry, music, love, friendship, hatred, passions, went on as always, independently and outside of any political closeness or enmity. . .and outside all possible reforms[107]

And though they find no content in that which they have, yet they cannot abide to hear of altering[108]

They often pull out their pencils at this point and make a note, under the belief that a tendency is portable[109]

He hath been blotted by some to be an Epitomist, that is, one that extinguished worthy whole volumes, to bring his abridgments into request[110]

Whatever his defects, a poet at least thinks a poem more important than anything which can be said about it[111]

But how shall men meditate in that, which they cannot understand?[112]

I will ask them a question about life. If they understand me—I will be saved; if they do not feel and understand me—I will be a poor miserable man, and I will suffer[113]

In his soul there suddenly arose such an unexpected tangle of youthful thoughts and hopes, contradictory to his whole life, that, feeling himself unable to comprehend his own state, he fell asleep at once[114]

What matters it to me if someone does not understand this? Let him too rejoice and say, "What is this?" Let him rejoice even at this, and let him love to find you while not finding it out, rather than, while finding it out, not to find you[115]

He opened the window. The night was fresh and stilly bright[116]

He opened a second window[117]

Whether it was respect, envy, or expectation—he did not know[118]

"No, life isn't over at the age of thirty-one. . .It's not enough that I know all that's in me, everyone else must know it, too. . . everyone must know me, so that my life is not only for myself. . .

but so that it is reflected in everyone, and they all live it together with me!"[119]

There were many chosen, that were greater in other men's eyes than their own, and that sought the truth rather than their own praise[120]

Again they came, or were thought to come, to the work[121]

The work hath not been huddled up[122]

A man feareth not the blame of convenient slackness[123]

"Hey, why're you always walking ahead of me?"
"Well, why you always walking behind me?"[124]

Suffering does not follow us. It goes before us[125]

And when Abram was ninety years old and nine, the Lord appeared to Abram, and said unto him, I am the Almighty God; walk before me, and be thou perfect[126]

He wanted so much to find in someone else the living ideal of that perfection for which he strove[127]

Better to be happy than wise[128]

Success is to be happy with the wise[129]

I wish to explain what God is, to everyone, but I will not if people start laughing[130]

Then Sarah denied, saying, I laughed not; for she was afraid. And he said, Nay; but thou didst laugh[131]

That be far from thee to do after this manner[132]

You are dead because your aims are death[133]

Let the dead bury their dead[134]

Nothing in the world is single[135]

He cannot love me that is afraid of me[136]

He is to thee a covering of the eyes[137]

Kutuzov turned away. The same smile of the eyes flashed over his face as when he had turned away from Captain Timokhin. He turned away and winced, as if wishing to express thereby that all that Dolokhov had said to him and all that he could say had long, long been known to him, that it all bored him, and that it was all by no means what was needed. He turned away and made for the coach[138]

Lord, wherefore hast thou so evil entreated this people? Why is it that thou hast sent me? For since I came to Pharoah to speak in thy name, he hath done evil to this people; neither hast thou delivered thy people at all[139]

And the tale of bricks, which they did make heretofore, ye shall lay upon them[140]

Getting back into bed, he cast around in his mind for something he desired to do that would injure no one, and he thought of skiing[141]

She could not fall asleep for a long time. She kept thinking that no one could understand all that she understood and all that was in her[142]

And the Lord said unto Moses, stretch out thine hand toward heaven, that there may be darkness over the land of Egypt, even darkness which may be felt[143]

She was sorry for herself, sorry that she had been going to waste for nothing, for nobody, all that while, throughout which she had felt herself capable of loving and of being loved[144]

She was in a state of remembrance[145]

Maybe he has come and is sitting there in the drawing room. Maybe he already came yesterday and I forgot[146]

After five minutes she felt terribly close to this man. Whenever she turned away, she was afraid he might take her bare arm from behind or kiss her on the neck[147]

Everything will be forgiven her, for she loved much; and everything will be forgiven him, for he had much fun[148]

Perhaps they wouldn't have forgiven her anyway, but it would have been for something different[149]

And the botanist who finds that the apple falls because the cellular tissue degenerates, and so on, will be as right and as wrong as the child who stands underneath and says that the apple fell because he wanted to eat it and prayed for it[150]

He may gape long ere a bird fall into his mouth[151]

We live among[152]

Too much explain[153]

He hath one eye in his neck[154]

A troop cometh[155]

This dreamer cometh[156]

This heap is a witness between me and thee this day[157]

And when he saw that he prevailed not against him, he touched the hollow of his thigh[158]

I will not let thee go, except thou bless me[159]

The sun rose upon him, and he halted upon his thigh[160]

And Esau said, I have enough, my brother; keep that thou hast unto thyself[161]

For an hundred pieces of money[162]

Do not interpretations belong to God?[163]

There was a certain creditor which had two debtors: the one owed five hundred pence and the other fifty. And when they had nothing to pay, he frankly forgave them both. Tell me therefore, which of them will love him most?[164]

I answer you according to your asking[165]

A man hath no more than he hath good of[166]

The quality of nothing hath not such need to hide itself[167]

For nothing is secret, that shall not be made manifest; neither anything hid, that shall not be known[168]

Take heed therefore how you hear: for whosoever hath, to him shall be given; and whosoever hath not, from him shall be taken even that which he seemeth to have[169]

Here's your money.
I didn't even count it[170]

For what is a man advantaged, if he gain the whole world, and lose himself[171]

1 Vaslav Nijinsky, *The Diary of Vaslav Nijinsky*, ed. (and trans.) Romola Nijinsky (Los Angeles: Simon and Schuster, 1936), 86.

2 Leo Tolstoy, *War and Peace*, trans. Richard Pevear and Larissa Volokhonsky (New York: Knopf, 2007), 422.

3 Antonio Porchia, *Voices*, trans. W.S. Merwin (Port Townsend: Copper Canyon, 2003), 125.

4 William Blake, "The Marriage of Heaven and Hell" in *The Complete Poetry and Prose,* ed. David V. Erdman (New York: Anchor Books, 1988), 37.

5 Ibid, "The Grey Monk," 489.

6 Nijinsky, *Diary,* 6.

7 Ibid, 11.

8 Martha Graham, *Blood Memory: An Autobiography* (New York: Doubleday, 1991), 13.

9 T.S. Eliot, *Four Quartets* (New York: Harcourt, Brace & World, 1943), 39.

10 Nijinsky, *Diary*, 3.

11 Ibid, 17.

12 Ibid, 3.

13 Jules Renard, *The Journal of Jules Renard*, trans. Louise Bogan and Elizabeth Roget, (Portland: Tin House, 2008), 284.

14 Martin Heidegger, *Early Greek Thinking* (New York: Harper and Row, 1975), 19.

15 Ibid.

16 Sir Thomas Wyatt, "My mother's maids when they did sew and spin," in *The Complete Poems*, ed. R.A. Rebholz (London: Penguin, 1978), 191.

17 Ibid.

18 Wallace Stevens, "Description without Place" in *The Palm at the End of the Mind*, ed. Holly Stevens (New York: Random House, 1967), 277.

19 Ibid, "Notes Toward a Supreme Fiction," 207.

20 Ibid, "The Dove in the Belly," 285.

21 Misspelled subtitle in a Godard film.

22 Eliot, *Four Quartets*, 25.

23 Jean-Luc Godard, interviewed by Dick Cavett, *The Dick Cavett Show*, 1980.

24 Ibid.

25 E.M. Forster, *Aspects of the Novel* (New York: Harcourt, 1955), 82.

26 Godard, *The Dick Cavett Show*.

27 Heidegger, *Early Greek Thinking*, 19.

28 J.D. Salinger, *Franny and Zooey* (New York: Little, Brown and Company, 1989), 122.

29 Renard, *The Journal*, 120.

30 Friedrich Nietzsche, "On Reading and Writing" in *Thus Spoke Zarathustra*, trans. Walter Kaufmann (New York: Penguin, 1966), 41.

31 Renard, *The Journal*, 104.

32 Erasmus, *Adagia in Latine and English* (London: Bernard Alsop, dwelling in Distaff-Lane at the signe of the Dolphine, 1621), 38.

33 J.D. Salinger, "Teddy," in *Nine Stories* (New York: Little, Brown and Company, 1981), 191.

34 Luke 10:3. All biblical citations refer to the King James translation.

35 Wyatt, "Mine own John Poyntz," *The Complete Poems*, 186.

36 Eliot, *Four Quartets*, 28.

37 Robert Frost, "Education by Poetry," in *Collected Poems, Prose & Plays*, ed. Richard Poirier and Mark Richardson (New York: Library of America, 1995), 726.

38 David Sylvester, *Interviews with Francis Bacon* (Oxford: Alden Press, 1980), 19.

39 Ibid, 21.

40 D.W. Winnicott, "The Capacity to Be Alone," in *The Maturational Processes and the Facilitating Environment* (New York: International Universities Press, 1965), 30.

41 Bacon/Sylvester, *Interviews*, 40.

42 Ibid, 43.

43 Renard, *The Journal*, 132.

44 Stevens, "Adagia" in *Opus Posthumous*, 188.

45 Renard, *The Journal*, 132.

46 Salinger, *Franny and Zooey*, 114.

47 Robert Browning, "'Childe Roland to the Dark Tower Came,'" in *Selected Poems*, ed. Daniel Karlin (London: Penguin, 1989), 99.

48 Salinger, *Franny and Zooey*, 133.

49 Ibid, 140.

50 Ibid, 143.

51 *A Midsummer Night's Dream*, ed. Richard Proudfoot et al. (London: Thomas Learning, 2001), 5.1.190.

52 James Wright, "The Young Good Man" in *Above the River: The Complete Poems* (New York: FSG, 1990), 231.

53 Ibid, "Son of Judas," 225.

54 Vladimir Nabokov, *Lolita* (New York: Random House, 1955), 15.

55 "Phaedo," trans. Benjamin Jowett, in *Harvard Classics,* Vol.II (New York: P.F. Collier & Son Corporation, 1937), 48.

56 Frost, "Poetry and School" in *Collected*, 808.

57 Porchia, *Voices*, 35.

58 Romola Nijinsky, preface to *The Diary of Vaslav Nijinsky*, xii-xiii.

59 Renard, *The Journal*, 109.

60 Porchia, *Voices*, 37.

61 Ibid, 35.

62 "The Golden Sayings of Epictetus," trans. Hastings Crossley, in *Harvard Classics,* Vol.II (New York: P.F. Collier & Son Corporation, 1937), 173.

63 Clarice Lispector, *Agua Viva*, trans. Stefan Tobler (New York: New Directions, 2012), 15.

64 Tom DeHaven and Joe Haldeman overheard on Norton Island, ME, July 2013.

65 Romans 11:6.

66 Frost, "Some Definitions," *Collected*, 701.

67 Eliot, *Four Quartets*, 32.

68 Paul Tillich, *The Courage to Be* (New Haven: Yale University Press, 1952), 25.

69 Tillich, *The Courage*, 25.

70 *The Golden Sayings of Epictetus*, 132.

71 Ibid, 131.

72 Ibid, 133.

73 Isak Dinesen, *Out of Africa and Shadows on the Grass* (New York: Vintage International, 1989), 7.

74 Cheever, "The Country Husband," *The Stories of John Cheever* (New York: Knopf, 1978), 393.

75 Frost, "On Taking Poetry," *Collected*, 825.

76 Frost, "Education by Poetry," *Collected*, 721.

77 *The Golden Sayings of Epictetus,* 147.

78 W.B. Yeats, "Who Goes with Fergus?" in *The Poems*, ed. Richard J. Finneran (New York: Macmillan, 1983), 43.

79 *The Golden Sayings of Epictetus*, 179.

80 Ibid, 169.

81 A.E. Housman, "The chestnut casts his flambeaux, and the flowers," in *The Works of A.E. Housman* (Ware: Wordsworth Editions, 1994), 108

82 "The Translators to the Reader," the 1611 version reproduced in *The Bible: Authorized King James Version*, ed. Robert Carroll and Stephen Prickett (Oxford: Oxford University Press, 1997), lxiii.

83 Renard, *The Journal*, 55.

84 Tolstoy, *War and Peace*, 4.

85 W.S. Merwin, introduction to *The Essential Wyatt* (New York: The Ecco Press, 1989), 11.

86 Tertullian, quoted in "The Translators to the Reader," lxiii.

87 Patricia Curd, introduction to *A Presocratics Reader* (Indianapolis: Hackett, 1996), 6.

88 "The Meditations of Marcus Aurelius," trans. George Long, in *Harvard Classics,* Vol.II (New York: P.F. Collier & Son Corporation, 1937), 279.

89 D.W. Winnicott, "Playing: A Theoretical Statement," in *Playing and Reality* (New York: Routledge, 1971), 50.

90 Nijinsky, *Diary*, 34.

91 Tolstoy, *War and Peace*, 25.

92 Genesis 4:23.

93 Ibid, 10:16-18.

94 *Wyatt*, 21.

95 Jackson C. Frank, *Blues Run the Game: Expanded Deluxe Version*, Sanctuary Records Group, 2002.

96 Nabokov, *Lolita*, 32.

97 Ralph Waldo Emerson, "Spiritual Laws," in *Emerson: Essays and Lectures* (New York: Library Classics of the United States, Inc., 1983), 316.

98 Walt Whitman, "Song of the Open Road," in *Leaves of Grass* (New York: Library of America, 1982), 303.

99 Winnicott, "The Capacity to Be Alone," in *Maturational Processes*, 30.

100 Erasmus*, Adagia*, 26.

101 Ibid, 30.

102 Ibid, 33.

103 Ibid, 37.

104 Winnicott, "Playing: A Theoretical Statement," *Playing and Reality*, 52.

105 Winnicott, "The Capacity to Be Alone," *Maturational Processes*, 31.

106 Tolstoy, *War and Peace*, 282.

107 Ibid, 418.

108 "The Translators to the Reader," lv.

109 Forster, *Aspects*, 28.

110 "The Translators to the Reader," liv.

111 W.H. Auden, "Making, Knowing and Judging, " *The Dyer's Hand* (New York: Random House, 1968), 49.

112 "The Translators to the Reader," lvi.

113 Nijinsky, *Diary*, 165.

114 Tolstoy, *War and Peace*, 422.

115 *The Confessions of St. Augustine*, trans. John K. Ryan (New York: Image Books, 1960), 48.

116 Tolstoy, *War and Peace*, 421.

117 Cheever, "The Country Husband," *The Stories*, 394.

118 Tolstoy, *War and Peace*, 428.

119 Ibid, 423.

120 "The Translators to the Reader," lxv.

121 Ibid.

122 Ibid, lxvi.

123 Ibid.

124 *Badlands*, dir. Terrence Malick, Warner Brothers, 1973.

125 Porchia, *Voices*, 39.

126 Genesis 17:1.

127 Tolstoy, *War and Peace*, 431.

128 Erasmus, *Adagia*, 3.

129 Wallace Stevens, from "Sur Plusieurs Beaux Subjects," in *Opus Posthumous*, ed. Milton J. Bates (New York: Knopf, 1989), 183.

130 Nijinsky, *Diary*, 50.

131 Genesis 18:15.

132 Genesis 18:25.

133 Nijinsky, *Diary*, 71.

134 *Luke* 9:60.

135 Shelley, "Love's Philosophy" in *A Book of Love Poetry*, ed. John Stallworthy (New York: Oxford University Press, 1973), 80.

136 Erasmus, *Adagia*, 20.

137 Genesis 20:16.

138 Tolstoy, *War and Peace*, 118.

139 Exodus 5:22-23.

140 Exodus 5:8.

141 Cheever, "The Country Husband," *The Stories*, 394.

142 Tolstoy, *War and Peace*, 452.

143 Exodus 10:21.

144 Tolstoy, *War and Peace*, 516-517.

145 Ibid, 518.

146 Ibid, 519.

147 Ibid, 565.

148 Ibid, 568.

149 Alice Munro, "The Children Stay," in *The Love of a Good Woman* (New York: Knopf, 1998), 214.

150 Tolstoy, *War and Peace*, 606.

151 Erasmus, *Adagia*, 23.

152 George Oppen, "Of Being Numerous," in *Collected Poems*, ed. Michael Davidson (New York: New Directions, 2002), 163.

153 T.S. Eliot, "Ash Wednesday," in *Let Us Go Then, You and I: Selected Poems* (London: Faber and Faber, 2009), 74.

154 Erasmus, *Adagia*, 20.

155 Genesis 30:11.

156 Genesis 37:19.

157 Genesis 31:48.

158 Genesis 32:25.

159 Genesis 32:26, and Dinesen, *Out of Africa*, 263.

160 Genesis 32:31.

161 Genesis 33:9.

162 Genesis 33:19.

163 Genesis 40:8.

164 Luke 7:41-42.

165 Erasmus, *Adagia*, 36.

166 Ibid, 24.

167 William Shakespeare, *King Lear*, ed. Louis B. Wright (New York: Washington Square Press, 1957), 1.2.34-35.

168 Luke 8:17.

169 Luke 8:18.

170 Wright, "Son of Judas," *Above the River*, 226.

171 Luke 9:25.

Notes

Sergei Kuzmich from All Sides: The de Kooning epigraph is from David Sylvester's *Interviews with American Artists*; the Tolstoy epigraph is from *War and Peace*, trans. Richard Pevear and Larissa Volokhonsky.

"Tractatus": The epigraph is from Flaubert's *Madame Bovary*, trans. Lydia Davis (2011 ed.).

"Assumed Knowledge and the Knowledge Assumed from Experience": The epigraph is from Nietzsche's *Thus Spake Zarathustra*, trans. Thomas Common.

"X-Men": The epigraph appears twice in the King James translation of Genesis (24:2, 47:29).

"Losss": The epigraph is from "The Golden Sayings of Epictetus," in *Harvard Classics*, Vol. II, trans. Hastings Crossley.

Acknowledgments

Thank you to the editors of the following publications in which some of these poems first appeared: *Atlantean Poets, Bennington Review, Boston Review, Company, Hyperallergic, The Iowa Review, Prelude, Two Peach, Typo,* and *The Volta*. Special thanks to Gale Nelson, who first published some of these poems in a chapbook, *He That Feareth Every Grass Must Not Piss in a Meadow*; and to the Catenary Press, who first published "Assumed Knowledge and the Knowledge Assumed from Experience" as a chapbook.

Thank you to Lisa Wells, Joshua Marie Wilkinson and Letter Machine Editions; to Boris Beric, Stephen Dunn, and Josip Novakovich; to Chelsea Gibson, Jana Benitez, Eliot D'Silva, James Galvin, Robert Hass, the members of Lyn Hejinian's Fall 2017 243B, Sarah Hymanson, Nadav Kurtz, Patrick LaBella, Mark Leidner, Mark Levine, Jessica O. Marsh, Jennifer Mazza, Daniel Miller, Geoffrey G. O'Brien, Bridget Talone, Alex Walton and Leonora Zoninsein.

Sara Deniz Akant, Jake Fournier, Callie Garnett, Daniel Poppick, Adrienne Raphel, Margaret Ross, Christian Schlegel – thank you. "Nothing. But nothing, literally, except my friends."

About the Author

Jessica Laser grew up in Chicago. A graduate of the Iowa Writers' Workshop, she has taught at Brown University, The University of Iowa, Manhattanville College, Parsons School of Design, and SUNY Purchase. She is pursuing a doctorate in English at The University of California, Berkeley. *Sergei Kuzmich from All Sides* is her first book.

Letter Machine Editions

Renee Angle, *WoO*
Cristiana Baik & Andy Fitch, editors,
The Letter Machine Book of Interviews
Anselm Berrigan, *To Hell With Sleep*
Edmund Berrigan, *Can It!*
Peter Gizzi, *Ode: Salute to the New York School*
Aaron Kunin, *Grace Period: Notebooks, 1998-2007*
Juliana Leslie, *More Radiant Signal*
Jessica Laser, *Sergei Kuzmich from All Sides*
Mark Levine, *Debt*
Farid Matuk, *This Isa Nice Neighborhood*
Fred Moten, *the feel trio*
Fred Moten, *the service porch*
Sawako Nakayasu, *Texture Notes*
Travis Nichols, *Iowa*
Alice Notley, *Benediction*
Andrea Rexilius, *Half of What They Carried Flew Away*
Andrea Rexilius, *New Organism: Essais*
Brandon Shimoda, *Evening Oracle*
Sara Veglahn, *Another Random Heart*
John Yau, *Bijioux in the Dark*
John Yau, *Exhibits*